HOME SERIES

HOME SERIES
SMALL SPACES

BETA-PLUS

CONTENTS

P. 4-5
A design by interior architect
Patric Deknock.

P. 6
A project by Olivier Dwek.
Decoration by Esther Gutmer.

FOREWORD

Ingenious, modular, multi-functional, tailor-made: these are the key words that crop up most often when people talk about small living areas.

Creating a sense of space in smaller properties can be a real challenge. All of the projects in this book have one thing in common: you quickly forget their limited dimensions. In fact, they often appear to be very spacious. It all comes down to the skill of the designer.

Interior architects are increasingly opening up these small spaces, rather than dividing them into different sections, and multifunctional rooms can be a very efficient way of gaining space. The classic dining room is often the first room to go, usually being incorporated into the kitchen.

Their small dimensions mean that these interiors are often more carefully designed and packed with useful features and tricks.

Many people are forced to live in a small space, but it can be a conscious choice.

More and more of us are opting for small city apartments and pieds à terre so that we don't have to give up on city life. The decision to live in a small property makes efficient use of the available space an absolute necessity.

This book presents sixteen projects featuring many useful, space-saving tips from inspirational designers and interior architects.

Their ideas are ingenious, but often very simple, and can transform a compact space into a pleasant and comfortable place to live.

P. 8
A project by the late Sophie Campion in a house designed by architect Baudouin Courtens.

P. 10-11
The dining room of antiques dealer Karim Grusenmeyer was inspired by the eighteenth century. An Italian 18th-century chandelier and a Louis XIV fireplace in French stone (late 17th century), an Italian column, a mirror with a large frame and two sculpted heads.

ALL IN ONE

O bumex created a large, open, multi-functional space in this apartment with modest dimensions. Work, relaxation, listening to music, a cosy dinner, even cooking – you can do it all in one single room.

The homogeneous character of the materials and colours results in a coherent and harmonious look. The room is semi-open; it has no doors, but a number of partitions to create a sense of rhythm, depth, and cosier spaces.

A good method that architects and landscape designers use to make a space appear larger is to create visual "breaks" to add variety and provide structure, so it is impossible to see the entire space at once.

A frosted glass screen separates the office and the TV room.

All of the furniture is from the Obumex collections.

P. 16-17
This small computer corner
can be closed off to create a
warm and cosy room around
the table.

A PENTHOUSE WITH ONE RESIDENT

I mmediately after completing her studies, Magali Van den Weghe was asked to redesign this thirty-year-old penthouse for a single female resident.

The client asked her to rejuvenate the space and bring it up to date.

Van den Weghe considered all of the details very carefully: she took down the walls and moved the pipes and cables to optimise the space and the light in the apartment. She also opted for clean lines and simple forms in sober materials, keeping the furniture limited so as not to overload the apartment. The property does not have large storage rooms to swallow up the space, but walls with shelves to accentuate horizontality and lightness.

The dining area consists of a long table and benches, so that there are no tall chair backs to block the view. The art by Muriel Emsens provides a colourful touch. An antique crystal chandelier.

Pure and simple lines ensure that the kitchen is not overloaded: matte cupboards (from MDC), floors and surfaces in Basaltina gris (Van den Weghe).

Another space-saving tip: extending the same floor throughout the entire area increases the sense of space.

In order to increase the impression of
space in this penthouse, the designer
removed the doorframes.

A WARM ATMOSPHERE

IN A FORMER SCULPTOR'S STUDIO

T he approach to a small living space does not always have to be hyper-modern.

This report features a simple project, a compact interior that is bursting with classic charm and sophistication.

This small studio with a vegetable garden was built amongst the fields in 1909. The owner Christine Lemaître thoroughly restored this house and turned it into a place of refuge, fizzing with life and far away from all of the noise and stress.

With her daughter Amélie de Borchgrave d'Altena, she selected all of the curtains and carpets, which emphasise the elegant and intimate atmosphere of this space: furniture, objects and paintings from different periods and places, with quality as the guiding principle. There are no imitations here.

This room has a rather contemporary atmosphere, combined with an old wooden floor. Left in the photograph, a large desk where everyone can check their email or leaf through a book. The wooden floor is from a 19th-century country house in Ireland. The desk is by Jules Wabbes; the chaise longue is by Charles Eames.

A view of the living room. The large sofa and armchair from Shabby Chic create a warm, informal atmosphere. The woven chair is by Wibo; rustic children's chairs from Sweden; old and contemporary paintings and drawings.

The patina on the wall is subtle and light, the result of layering the paint (Chintz Shop). A cosy setting, accentuated by the faded colours of the Shabby Chic linen fabrics. Paintings by Yves Zurstrassen (centre) and Peter Gutierrez (right).

The colours of the small sitting room were inspired by Masaccio's frescos in Florence. The blind is in a fabric used for tents by nomads in northern Pakistan.

A Louis XVI desk and a cane Regency-period armchair. The linen curtains are from Shabby Chic.

A SMALL LOFT

AND A TOUCH OF ILLUSION

I nterior architect Marc Thoen designed this private apart- ment with a terrace, above a shop.

Most of the exterior wall was demolished to create a direct connection between the living area and the terrace. The light metal structure of the windows and the wooden floors, which extend both inside and outside, create an open and spa- cious feeling.

The result is a very contemporary look. Dark wood, white walls, large metal win- dows with an industrial feel, designer furniture: all of these elements underline the zen minimalism of this project.

Two storage spaces have been discreetly incorporated beside the custom-made fireplace, which runs on both gas and coal. The whole structure rests on a suspended concrete surface, which was hand-finished in situ. Maxalto salon, Sity B&B. Lighting by Delta Light. The broad oak wooden planks have an oiled finish.

The entrance to the living room is a sliding door that occupies the entire width of the corridor. An extra-long table by Maxalto. Zanotta chairs and a Sity armchair by B&B.

Like the terrace, the kitchen (designed by Grando) was opened up to become part of a single space.
In spite of the rather limited dimensions, the simplicity of materials and colours creates a sense of space in this apartment. All of the storage space is behind the large electric sliding panel. Barstools: Mobles 114 Barcelona.

A COMPACT HOLIDAY HOME

ON THE CÔTE D'AZUR

L imited dimensions, but an ingenious use of space: this apartment in Cannes is only 100m^2, but offers all the comforts you need for a holiday visit.

White walls, blond wood: a winning combination for creating a sense of space in this modern interior.

P. 34-37
Sphere Home Interiors created a gentle atmosphere by combining all of the living functions in one harmonious whole: work, relaxation, watching television, eating. Poufs in suede and a Meridiani sofa. Art by An Selen.
Kitchen chairs also by Meridiani.

The cane outdoor furniture is by Sempre.

The kitchen was created to a Sphere design. The pots on the kitchen work surface are by Vincent Van Duysen for When Objects Work.

Beds by Olivier Strelli for Beka and poufs by Marie's Corner. Linen bedclothes by Gwendolino and lighting by Stéphane Davidts.

The bathroom, also a design by Sphere, is in marble mosaic. Dornbracht taps.

A SMALL, VERTICAL LOFT

T he industrial site of the Gevaert weaving mill has been part of Thomas Gevaert's world since he was born.
When he was studying architecture, he inherited one of the three worker's homes on this listed site.

The protected facade had to remain intact, but Gevaert completely changed the layout of the interior. He replaced the two upper floors, which originally had high ceilings, with three levels with ceilings of a standard height, thereby creating more floor space.

As the three floors no longer corresponded with the windows of the original house, he installed a staircase inside the front of the building to accommodate both the windows and the new layout.

A warm loft atmosphere in this space, where the use of deep purple on some of the walls gives the whole a sense of depth, coherence and character.

The stairs run along the walls, parallel to the different living zones.

The living areas are on the upper floors to give more of a sense of space and better light.

Stairs, kitchen and dining area on the second floor.
By omitting walls and treating the stairs as a decorative element, he has created a connection between all of the floors, so that this space seems like a vertical loft.

The bedroom, bathroom and garden are on the ground floor.

A SOBER STYLE

WITH MARITIME ACCENTS

S and's Company furnished this small sea-view apartment. Demyttenaere architectural studio coordinated the building works.

This holiday home was designed in a sober, contemporary style with a number of maritime accents. All of the walls are painted white and the apartment has a magnificent sea view, which creates a great sense of space, in spite of the limited floor area.

The interior design is based around the connection between inside and outside. The use of large sliding doors creates the necessary sense of cosiness.

MDF cupboard painted white with a special detail: the handles are from a range designed for boats.
Parquet in bleached oak; shelves and table in oak. On the ceiling, built-in adjustable spotlights. To the right of the cupboard, floor spotlights.

The kitchen is completely separate from the rest of the apartment. The glass sliding door allows a perfect view of the sea.

In the kitchen, the designers opted for floors and kitchen work surfaces in rough granite. A glass wall beside the cooking area.

Storage space, toilets and a bathroom are concealed behind the curved wall.

Mirrored cabinets above the washbasins. Floor, surface and bath surround in granite.

Steam shower with a granite floor and walls in Basaltina.

CONTEMPORARY ART

AND INDIVIDUAL SPACES

I n her private apartment, Marie-Paule De Vil (Geukens & De Vil) displays a number of works by artists who are also exhibited in her gallery.

This art historian convincingly demonstrates how contemporary art can be harmoniously integrated in a timeless and very individual interior.

Above the sofa, a work in gold leaf by Renaat Ivens.
Right, the work *Two Stone* by Anna-Eva Bergman, the wife of Hans Hartung.

To the right of the open fireplace, a photograph by artist and performer Zhang Huan, exiled from China and now living in New York.

P. 54-55
Above the sofa, a work by Marie-Jo Lafontaine, *À fleur du mal*. In spite of the limited amount of space, the designer chose a daring shade of purple that gives this project a mysterious and intimate appeal.

Two works from the oeuvre of photographer Peter Lindbergh: a nude of Nadja Auermann and a portrait of Marie-Sophie Wilson.

A kitchen and dining area in plain, white shades. On the wall, *A Bottle of Water*, a 1993 work by Peter Lindbergh.

A COMPACT WHOLE

T his compact total concept by interior architect Filip Vanryckeghem, created by Interieur Vandeputte, is the product of lengthy discussion with the owners.

The result: a setting in which the limited amount of space is perceived as pleasant and functional.

The volumes have been optimised: built-in storage space discreetly incorporated into the walls. The sober, masculine style of the decoration has been extended into all of the rooms: furniture in dark wood, in simple and streamlined designs.

This consistent approach throughout the project makes the space appear larger. There are no interruptions to the decoration: everything flows seamlessly together.

The open character of this apartment is clear from the moment you step into the entrance hall, which leads straight into the living space.

The very practical dining area was designed to make optimal use of the space:
the bench against the wall ensures that no space is wasted.

Decoration and curtains by Domus. Paintwork by A. Vanwalleghem.

The designer opted for an open kitchen, close to the table and the reception room.

To emphasise the harmony throughout this project, the same materials have been used in the bathroom, toilets and kitchen: lacquered glass and Corian surfaces.

A glass screen separates the entrance hall and the living room.

A REJUVENATED CITY HOME

This city house with modest dimensions had a lot of negative points to start with: it was dark and gloomy, with lots of very small bedrooms.

This was a real challenge for Pas-Partoe Interieur, who transformed this sad house into a modern home that is light and airy.

In collaboration with Karel Beeck, who supervised the structural work, the designers removed some of the internal walls to create a spacious living room along the whole length of the ground floor.

A tip for gaining space: combine the kitchen and dining room in one elegant zone. The folding doors and outdoor lighting make the garden feel like part of the interior. All of the doors are ceiling height and obtrusive elements, such as radiators and speakers, are camouflaged. The few large pieces of furniture create a strong sense of space. The contrasts in style, shape and colour reinforce the character of this home.

The living room is next to the kitchen/dining room. A custom-made armchair, a carpet in astrakhan wool, a corner unit and a Minotti pouf. The white painted blinds are mounted invisibly.

In the background, Gandia Blasco garden furniture. The dining room chairs and the J. Morrison lighting contrast with the geometric design of the dining table in American walnut wood. The bench is by Bataille & ibens. The kitchen appliances are concealed behind sliding doors. The wide bleached pine planks are from Canada.

A music system and a CD collection have been incorporated within the TV unit.

Obumex fitted the Pawson kitchen/ dining room.

A view of the parents' bedroom with a lamp by Marcel Wanders.
Door handles in nickel-plated brass with a brushed finish. The original wooden floor (ca. 400 years old) has been restored.

An Orizzoni bed, a Bataille & ibens sofa and a T07 wardrobe.

The children's bedroom: floor with MDF panels in tongue and groove, protected by six layers of varnish. Stairs in sisal carpeting.

The open bathroom, with fitted cupboards and washbasins by Vincent Van Duysen.

An open shower in a built-in alcove. Boffi taps. The asymmetric design of the washbasins, the lighting directed at the white washbasin and the ceiling-height doors increase the sense of space in this compact room.

THE TRANSFORMATION

OF A BUNGALOW
INTO A CONTEMPORARY HOME

I nterior architect Philip Simoen was asked to transform this 1960s bungalow into a contemporary home for a young couple.

In spite of the limited amount of volume, Philip Simoen succeeded in creating a sense of openness and space in the new design concept. The interior now has a minimalist loft atmosphere. Most of the space has been opened up; white walls, rough and natural materials and design furniture have brought about a real metamorphosis.

The living room in the old section. Armchairs in black leather from Zanotta.
Modular lighting and a vintage lamp from the 1970s.
Red table and bench, Picnik by Xavier Lust for Extremis.

The kitchen, custom-built in white
Formica and wengé to a design by
Philip Simoen, is in the new extension.
Smeg appliance.
Plastic chairs around a specially made
dining table in stainless steel. Modular
lighting. A long light well separates the
old construction from the new section.

A double-sided open fireplace
separates the living room from the
kitchen. Modular lighting and rocking
chairs by Eames for Vitra.

The former attic has been made into a bedroom, dressing room and bathroom, with fitted MDF units. The shower room is in 2x2cm glass mosaic tiles by Bisazza. Aktiva taps by Grohe. A custom-built steel staircase by Feys.

The bathroom is in white glass mosaic by Bisazza (2x2 cm). Fitted sink unit, Axor taps and Duravit washbasin.

LIGHT AND SPACE

IN A CLASSIC INTERIOR

T his small apartment has been tastefully furnished with Orac's decorative range. Classic cornices and skirting, with a white paint finish or in natural wood, give any interior an extra touch of class and restfulness.

The many windows ensure that this is a light and airy space, all year round.

The skirting, cornices and ceiling moulding in this dining room/kitchen are from a range by Orac. Gustavian-style dining room and chairs.

A pale wood was selected for the wall unit, with a classic cornice from the Orac Decor collection.

The apartment is bathed in light, so the pale paint and woods are a natural choice.

The bedroom is finished with a panel based on a skirting design from the Orac Axxent collection and moulding by Orac Decor. Here, a simple cornice with built-in spotlights.

MODERNISM AND SERENITY

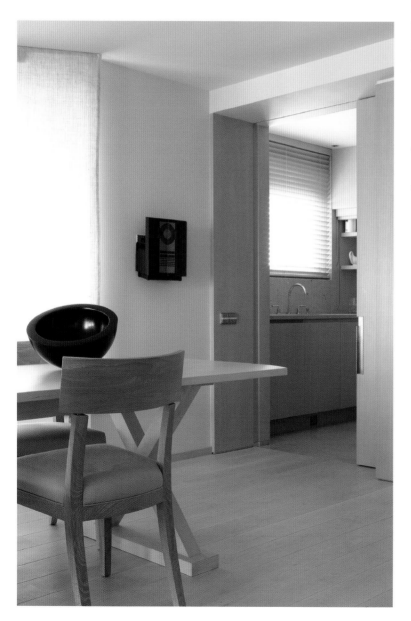

For over thirty years, Obumex have combined technological sophistication with a passion for pure design. For every aspect of home design, the company offers an aesthetic solution created with top-quality materials.

This report features two projects by Obumex that are perfect illustrations of their approach.

In this first project, a holiday home by the sea, the intention was to reflect the shades of the sea and the sand. The designers selected a sand-coloured parquet floor and ceiling-height panels that continue through the dining room and kitchen, entrance hall and bedrooms, creating a sense of continuity in this cosy holiday setting with a sea view.

The art from the gallery of Patrick De Brock was an appropriate choice. The colours add a splash of sunlight to this subtle mix of neutral shades.

A young and lively atmosphere in the children's rooms, with orange walls and lights in aluminium frames. A fine example of the dynamic within this project: the grey sliding door that leads to the shower.

In this second project, Obumex created a symbiosis between the classic modern furniture by Promemoria and the most minimalist of kitchens: Pawson by Obumex.
Introducing a warm red-brown variety of wood has created a cosy atmosphere in the kitchen, an effect that is reinforced by the table in the bay window and the deep shades of the TV corner.

The main room consists of a breakfast area, two small seating spaces and an office (Promemoria and Christian Liaigre) on different levels. The oak floors are in an anthracite shade throughout. Although this is a square room, the different zones are clearly defined by the subtle colour combinations and the different varieties of wood. The office provides an atmosphere where you can work in peace, while still remaining at the heart of the home.

TIMELESS STYLE

IN A SIMPLE COUNTRY HOUSE

T his house with a view of a meadow landscape is the result of close collaboration between Porte Bonheur and Natalie Haegeman Interiors.

Ingrid Segers and Annemie Coppens, the founders of Porte Bonheur, constructed this country house, using reclaimed materials in a timeless style.

NH-Interiors then decorated and furnished the interior, in a warm and cosy atmosphere.

In order to gain space, they integrated the dining room within the kitchen, a layout that is often found in contemporary interiors, but which is clearly catching on in more classic interiors too.

The narrow entrance hall is streamlined simplicity itself.
The walls and staircase have been plastered and the stairs are finished in oak. The doors and the small staircase down to the cellar are in old pine. The cement floor also adds to the sober look of the whole.

An oak floor in the living room.

The walls of the TV room have been painted with a limewash that was mixed on the spot, as was the case throughout the house. In spite of the limited amount of space, the designers opted for a dark raspberry colour in this room, which creates a cosy oriental atmosphere. A coffee table with an oak surface (19th century) and a wrought-iron base.
Two small, symmetrically positioned aluminium windows at the back of the room.

As in all of the rooms, the dining room has old pine doors with authentic handles.
The old pine desk with an original red patina is from Hungary.

An old terracotta floor (a mixture of red and black tiles) in the annexe and the washing room. Custom-made doors in old pine. The small bluestone washbasin has a pedal pump.

The kitchen cupboards are in oak. The floor is in old terracotta tiles. The kitchen work surface was treated and given a painted finish. A raised open fireplace and whitewashed walls. The table and the old bench in painted wood effect are from Hungary. The cushions are made from old kilims.

Old oak shutters separate the corridor from the dining room. Tailor-made lamps in beautiful fabrics.

The upstairs hall is simply designed, but has a warm atmosphere.

An oak floor and meticulously restored oak beds, finished in velvet. The old oak worktable functions as a side table. A kilim on the floor.

This Italian-inspired bathroom and shower are in tadelakt. The concrete sink has a special finish.

CONTEMPORARY ELEGANCE

G illes de Meulemeester and his design studio Ebony furnished this small apartment in dark shades and sober, luxurious, contemporary materials with a timeless touch.

This project is true to Gilles de Meulemeester's philosophy: an ethnic touch combined with contemporary streamlined elegance. This is a minimalist look that has a warm atmosphere because of the use of dark shades of wood.

The oak panels conceal the lift and service rooms.

Custom-made wall units by Ebony. An Edouardo coffee table in anthracite-grey oak.

A diptych by Christine Nicaise.

A Dumbo table and Marella chairs, both in anthracite-tinted oak.
A sideboard with doors and drawers in palisander wood, a striped wool carpet, a console in steel and wengé.

Right in the photo, a work of art by Florimond Dufoor. Ceiling light in wengé-tinted oak and bronze.

The dressing room is in tinted oak, facing a set of windows.

Custom-made bedclothes in linen and silk.
A foldaway bedside table in mahogany. Art
by Ela Tom.

A BOLD RENOVATION

IN A HISTORIC SETTING

T his project by Kempen-based company Antiques & Design is a fine example of their expertise: a harmony of old and new elements, combined with contemporary living comfort in a classic setting.

The bold use of colour, the unusual fabrics and the decorative wallpaper give the project an exuberant and distinctive look.

The combination of the client's wishes and the creative ideas of the Antiques & Design team, combined with the use of unique historic elements, has created a very personal and flamboyant interior.

Antiques & Design create complete interiors: from design to completion.
The shade of blue gives this country-style kitchen a lively touch.

VARIETIES
OF INTERNAL
TORMENT

HOME SERIES

Volume 7 : SMALL SPACES

The reports in this book are selected from the Beta-Plus collection of home-design books: www.betaplus.com
They have been compiled in a special series by Le Figaro in French language: Ma Déco

Copyright © 2009 Beta-Plus Publishing / Le Figaro
Originally published in French language

PUBLISHER
Beta-Plus Publishing
Termuninck 3
B – 7850 Enghien
Belgium
www.betaplus.com
info@betaplus.com

PHOTOGRAPHY
Jo Pauwels

DESIGN
Polydem - Nathalie Binart

TRANSLATIONS
Laura Watkinson

ISBN: 9789089440389

Printed in China

P. 122-123
A fireplace in Pietra Piasentina with Gucci accessories and two photographs by
Jean-Loup Sieff. Club chairs and a square padded Minotti pouf in foal skin that
serves as a coffee table. A project by Guy Stapels interior consultancy.

P. 124-125
Sleeping in an alcove means saving space: the home of antiques dealer Rik Mahieu.
The floor is in old planks.

P. 126-127
This kitchen was created by Obumex.